Investigating Science

How do we use materials?

Jacqui Bailey

W
FRANKLIN WATTS
LONDON • SYDNEY

First published in 2005 by Franklin Watts
96 Leonard Street, London EC2A 4XD

Franklin Watts Australia
45–51 Huntley Street, Alexandria, NSW 2015

Series editor: Rachel Cooke
Editor: Jennifer Schofield
Design: Rachel Hamdi/Holly Mann
Picture researcher: Diana Morris
Photography: Ray Moller, unless otherwise acknowledged

Acknowledgements:
Peter Frost/Topham: front cover ct. Houghton/Topham: 24t.
Picturepoint/Topham: 21t, 26clb.

With thanks to our models: Alexandra Baille, Carlo Anderson,
Shani-è Cox, Ben Treasure, Amber Harris, Donald Selmani

Every attempt has been made to clear copyright.
Should there be any inadvertent omission please
apply to the publisher for rectification.

A CIP catalogue record for this book
is available from the British Library.

ISBN: 0 7496 6093 7

Printed in Malaysia

Contents

What are materials?

Materials are the substances that things are made of. Your clothes are made from a group of materials called **fabrics**. But everything else in the world is made from materials, too.

THINK about all the different materials there are.
- The chair you are sitting on might be made of wood or plastic.
- This book is made from paper.

What other types of material can you see around you?

You will need:

A sheet of paper ✔

A pencil and a ruler ✔

A group of objects made from different materials (e.g. your school bag and all the objects inside it) ✔

What are things made of?

(1) Use the pencil and ruler to draw a line down the middle of the paper.

(2) In the left-hand column, make a list of all the different objects you have.

(3) In the right-hand column, write down the materials you think each object is made of.

(4) Remember that some objects, such as a pencil, may be made from more than one material. Ask an adult if you are not sure what a material is called.

(5) How many materials did you find? In each case, why was that material used and not another?

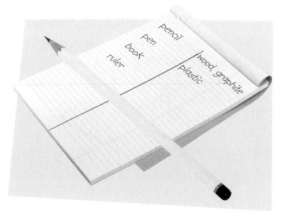

Because . . .

We use so many different materials because each one behaves in a slightly different way — it has different properties. Nylon, a type of plastic, is strong and bendy so it is used to make ropes. Metal is strong and stiff, so we use it to make spoons.

Hard or soft?

Some materials are hard and strong. Some are soft and squishy. We use them in different ways.

THINK about your bed. Which parts of it are hard and which are soft?

- The legs and frame are made of a hard material.
- The mattress is a mixture of soft padding and hard, bouncy springs.
- The sheets are soft and floppy.

What materials are the hard and soft parts made from?

You will need:

A sheet of paper ✔

A pencil and a ruler ✔

Which materials are hard and which are soft?

1 Use the ruler to divide your paper into four columns and head them as shown.

2 Look at the objects in a room — your bedroom, for example. List all the objects in the first column, and the materials they are made from in the second.

3 Is each material hard or soft? Put a tick in the 'hard' column or the 'soft' column for each object. Why do you think that, for some objects, hard materials were used instead of soft materials?

Because . . .

Hard materials, such as metal and wood, are useful because they are strong and keep their shape. They are good for building with or for supporting weight, so we use them to make furniture. Soft materials bend and wrap around different shapes, so we use them to make comfortable clothes and bedding.

Stretch and squeeze

Some materials are **elastic**. This means that they can be pulled or squashed into different shapes. Then, when you let them go, they snap back into their original shape.

THINK about some things that are elastic.

- A sponge squashes.
- An elastic band stretches.
- Lots of clothes are stretchy.

Find out more about stretchy fabrics.

You will need:
A sheet of paper ✔
A pencil and a ruler ✔
A selection of different clothes (e.g. a pair of tights, a woolly hat, a T-shirt, a raincoat, a swimsuit) ✔

Which fabrics are the stretchiest?

1 Divide your paper into three columns. Name your columns: 'clothing', 'stretch' and 'material'.

2 Write the names of your test clothes in the first column.

3 Tug on each piece of clothing to test it for stretchiness. Mark it 1 for no stretch, 2 for some stretch and 3 for lots of stretch.

clothing	stretch	material
t-shirt	2	cotton
hat	2	wool
tights	3	lycra/nylon
raincoat	1	

4 Now check the labels inside each piece of clothing to see what materials it is made from. Write down the materials in the third column. Which fabrics are the stretchiest?

Because . . .

Some fabrics stretch more than others because they are made from a mixture of materials. Some of the stretchiest fabrics include a material called Elastane Lycra. This material lets fabrics stretch and return to shape. The more a fabric stretches, the more Elastane Lycra it has in it.

Does it bend?

Some materials bend, but others do not. Bendy materials are called **flexible**. Materials that do not bend easily are described as **rigid**.

THINK about things that are bendy and things that are not.

• Cotton thread is very flexible and good for sewing things together.

• A sewing needle made from metal is rigid, so it can push through fabric.

Which materials are flexible and which are not?

You will need:

A selection of different materials (e.g. a drinking straw, a wooden pencil, a piece of string, a birthday-cake candle, paper, a metal coat-hanger, a metal spoon, a plastic fork, a spatula) ✔

A pencil and a sheet of paper ✔

Which materials are bendy?

1 Starting with the drinking straw, try to bend each object.

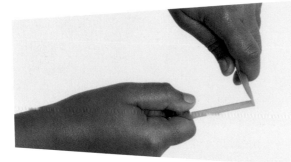

2 Note down the materials that bend easily, those that are hard to bend, and those that break!

3 Make a list of the reasons why you think we need bendy materials and why we need stiff materials.

4 Compare your list with a friend's.

Because . . .

Flexible materials are useful because we can bend or fold them into any shape we want. Rigid materials are useful because they keep their shape when you use them. Some rigid materials are very strong, but others break easily when we bend them. We say these materials are **brittle**.

THINK about using:
- Wood to make shoelaces.
- Paper to make a stepladder.

What do you think would happen?

Shiny or dull?

Some materials are shiny and some are dull.

THINK about how some materials **reflect** (bounce back) more light than others. Which materials reflect the most light?

shiny

What makes materials shiny?

(1) Look around a room. How many things can you find that reflect light? What materials are they made from?

(2) Now look for objects that do not reflect light. What materials are they made from?

(3) Make lists of your shiny and dull materials and compare them. Which materials are smooth and which are rough?

Because . . .

Smooth, polished materials shine the most because more light bounces straight off them. Rough materials scatter light, so they look dull.

dull

THINK about what happens when a smooth surface becomes dusty. Is it still shiny?

You will need:
Aluminum foil ✔
Some butter ✔

What makes materials dull?

1 Carefully cut a piece of foil and look at its shinier side. Can you see your reflection in it?

2 Now crumple up the foil and roughly straighten it out again. What happens?

3 Smear some butter on another piece of foil. Is it still as shiny as it was?

Because . . .

The foil was shiniest when it was smooth and clean because it reflected the light well. We use materials that reflect light well to make mirrors. Mirrors are made by placing a smooth piece of glass on top of a thin layer of shiny metal.

See through?

Some materials are **transparent** – we can see right through them. Some are **opaque** – this means we cannot see through them at all. Other materials are **translucent** – things look blurry through them.

THINK about things that are transparent, opaque and translucent.

- Clear glass is transparent.
- Most clothes are opaque!
- Net curtains are translucent.

Look at some materials and decide how much you can see through them.

You will need:

A cardboard tube (e.g. the inner tube from a roll of toilet paper) ✔

Sticky tape or elastic bands ✔

Test materials (e.g. paper, cotton cloth, a tissue, cling film, a plastic bag, metal foil, tracing paper, felt, sweet wrapper) ✔

A pencil and paper ✔

Which materials can you see through?

1 Hold the cardboard tube up to one eye, like a telescope, and check that you can see clearly through it.

2 Wrap each test material in turn over one end of the tube. Hold the test material in place with sticky tape or elastic bands. Look through the tube to discover if you can see through the material.

3 Which test materials can you see through? Is what you see clear or fuzzy?

4 Make a list of which test materials are transparent, which are translucent and which are opaque.

Because . . .

Transparent materials, such as glass and clear plastic, are useful because light can pass through them but other things cannot. Glass windows let light into a building but they keep out the rain. Clear plastic storage containers allow us to see what is inside them without having to open them.

Waterproof?

Some materials are **waterproof** – liquids roll off them. But other materials are **absorbent** – liquids soak into them.

THINK about what happens when it is raining.

- Rain runs off a stone pavement.
- Rain soaks into the soil.

What waterproof materials can you think of?

You will need:

An empty plastic tumbler ✔
A jug of water ✔
Some test materials (e.g. kitchen towel, cling film, aluminium foil, cotton cloth, a plastic bag) ✔
A large plastic bowl ✔
A wax candle ✔
Elastic bands ✔

Is it waterproof?

1. Half fill the tumbler with water.

2. Wrap each piece of material in turn over the top of the tumbler and hold it tightly in place with the elastic bands.

3. Turn the tumbler upside down over the bowl. What happens with each material?

Because . . .

Waterproof materials are useful because they allow us to keep things dry, and to store and carry liquids. Absorbent materials are useful for cleaning things or rubbing them dry.

THINK about the clothes you wear in the rain. Unlike most of your clothes, they are waterproof. Often an extra material is added to the fabric.

Can you make it waterproof?

(1) Rub a candle over a dry piece of cotton cloth so that it becomes well waxed (you might need an adult to help you soften the candle a little).

(2) Now put the cloth over the tumbler of water, as before, waxed side out. Does the candle wax make a difference?

Float or sink?

Some things float easily in water, and some do not.

Find out which materials float and which materials sink.

Will it float or sink?

1. Make a list of your objects and note down which ones you think will sink and which will float.

2. Put them in the water one at a time and see if you were right.

3. Make a note of those objects that float, and those objects that sink straight to the bottom. Are the objects that sink similar in any way?

Because . . .

Small, heavy objects, such as metal coins and glass marbles, sink straight to the bottom. Materials such as wood and cork float because they are light for their size and waterproof. An absorbent material, such as a piece of kitchen towel, may float to begin with, but then it soaks up water and sinks.

THINK about a large ship
- It is made from metal, just like a coin.
- It is a very different shape from a coin.

Do you think the ship's shape helps it to float?

Can you make it float?

1. Try floating a lump of Plasticine. Then pat it dry.

2. Roll it out into a wide, flat shape. Fold up the sides a little to make a boat shape.

3. Now carefully place it on the water. Does it float or sink?

Hot or cold?

Heat travels easily through some materials. These materials warm up more quickly than others.

THINK about how heat travels from a hot material to a colder one when someone makes you a hot drink.

- The hot liquid heats up the cold cup.
- The heat travels into the air around the cup and the liquid and they become cooler. Soon you can pick up the cup, and drink the liquid.

Can you see heat travel from one material to another?

You will need:

A wooden spoon, a metal spoon and a plastic spoon, all the same length ✔

Some butter ✔

3 peas ✔

A heatproof jug ✔

A saucepan of hot water ✔

An adult to help ✔

How can you see heat travel?

1 Use a small knob of butter to glue one pea to the end of each spoon handle.

2 Carefully stand the three spoons upright in the jug, with the peas at the top.

3 Ask an adult to pour a little hot water into the base of the jug, no deeper than the bowls of the spoons.

4 Which pea is the first one to fall? Which is the last?

Because . . .

*The peas fell off because heat from the water travelled up the spoons and melted the butter. The pea fell off the metal spoon first because heat travels quickly through metal. We say that metal is a good **conductor** of heat.*

THINK about a metal pan with a wooden handle.

● Metal heats up quickly so that food will cook.

● The wood stays cool so the cook can pick up the pan.

We call a material that heat travels through slowly an **insulator**.

Made by nature

Many of the materials we use are **natural materials** — they come from living things, or from the Earth itself.

THINK about how many natural materials there are.

- Wood used for furniture and buildings comes from trees.
- Clay and sand come from the earth and rocks.
- Wool used for knitting and weaving cloth comes from sheep.

How can you make a piece of wool into a piece of cloth?

How does wool make cloth?

1 Cut small triangular teeth into the two longest edges of the cardboard. You may need an adult to help you with this.

2 Loop one colour wool around one end of the board and tie a knot. Wind the wool along the card so that each loop sits in one of the teeth (see page 25). This is called the warp thread.

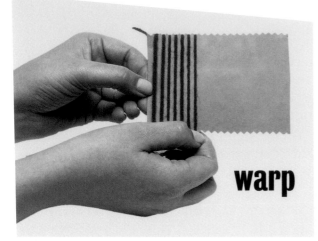

warp

weft

3 Thread the needle with the other colour wool. Use the needle to pull the wool under and over each of the warp threads. At the end of one row, turn the needle around and work back in the opposite direction. This is the weft thread.

4 As you do each row, push it up gently so that it sits closely to the row next to it.

5 When you have filled one side of the cardboard, knot the end of your weft thread. Then cut along the middle of the warp threads on the back of the cardboard and take your woven cloth off it.

Because . . .

Natural materials are useful because we can make all kinds of things from them. Sometimes we change a material's shape, such as turning a fleece into woollen yarn. We can also break up a material, such as by chopping wood. But the material itself does not change.

Making materials

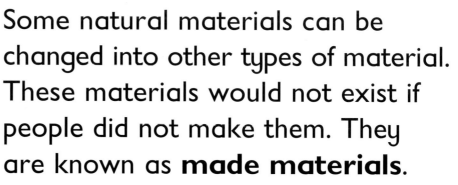

Some natural materials can be changed into other types of material. These materials would not exist if people did not make them. They are known as **made materials**.

THINK about how we change natural materials into made materials.

- Sand is heated up and turned to glass.
- Clay is shaped, baked and glazed to make china.
- Oil is used to make all kinds of plastics, such as polythene, polyester and nylon.
- Wood is chopped and then boiled to make paper.

There are many ways to change one material into another.

You will need:

A block of modelling clay ✔

A rolling pin ✔

A strip of card about 5 cm wide and 50 cm long ✔

Plaster of Paris powder ✔

A clean jug ✔

Water ✔

Can you make a soft material into a hard one?

① Roll out the clay into a round, flat base, at least 1 cm thick and a little bigger than your hand.

② Press your flat hand firmly into the clay. Lift up your hand so that you leave its shape printed in the clay.

③ Curve the strip of card into a circle that fits around your hand print. Press it gently into the clay so that it stays in place.

④ Put some plaster of Paris in the jug and mix it with water until you have a creamy paste.

⑤ Pour the paste into the card circle so that it completely covers the hand print. Leave the paste to dry.

⑥ When the paste is completely dry, peel away the clay and the card. You are left with a hard plaster model of your hand.

Because . . .

The plaster of Paris changed from a soft powder into a hard plaster because it was mixed with water and left in the open air. Many materials are changed by mixing them with other materials. Sometimes they change when they are heated.

Useful words

Absorbent materials, such as sponges and paper tissues, soak up liquids.

Brittle materials are hard, but they shatter or break easily if they are bent or smashed. Glass and china are both brittle materials.

Conductors are materials that allow heat to pass through them easily. They heat up and cool down quickly. Metals are good conductors.

Materials that absorb
Some materials do not just absorb water, they also soak up other things. A thick, dark cloth will absorb heat, light and sound.

Elastic materials are stretchy and springy. These materials can be pulled or squashed out of their original shape, but return to it when they are let go. Rubber and Elastane Lycra are elastic materials.

Fabrics are the cloths we make from different materials. Cotton, woollen and nylon cloth are all fabrics.

Flexible materials are easily bent and folded. Unlike elastic materials, they do not naturally return to their original shape. Paper, copper wire and some plastics are flexible.

Insulators are materials that do not allow heat to pass through them easily. Insulators can be used to keep heat in or out. Wood and some plastics are good insulators.

28

Made materials are materials that have been produced by people. Paper and plastics are made.

Natural materials grow from living things or are part of the Earth itself. Wood, oil and rock are all natural materials.

Opaque materials do not allow any light to pass through them. Most materials are opaque, so we cannot see through them.

Reflection happens when light bounces off the surface of a material. If the surface is very smooth, it **reflects** light and we can sometimes see an image of ourselves or other objects in it.

Rigid materials cannot bend or fold. Wood is a rigid material.

Translucent materials allow some light to pass through them but they also reflect some light. You can see through them but only in a blurry way. Tracing paper is translucent.

Transparent materials allow light to pass through them. Colourless glass, water and some plastics are transparent. You can see through them.

Waterproof materials do not soak up liquids. Instead, liquids stay on the surface of the material and cannot pass through it. Materials such as metal, glass and some plastics are waterproof.

Words for made materials

Another word for materials that are made is artificial. We also say some made materials are synthetic. Synthetic materials are made in factories by mixing and heating chemicals. Some fabrics are synthetic.

Index